Do not worry about your life, what you will eat or drink, or about your body, what you will wear. Is not life more important than food, and the body more important than clothes? Look at the birds of the air; they do not sow or reap or store away in barns, and yet your heavenly Father feeds them. Are you not much more valuable than they? Who of you by worrying can add a single hour to his life?

Original edition published in English under the title *Do Not Worry*
by Lion Publishing, plc, Oxford, England. Copyright © Lion Publishing, 2001.
North American edition published by Good Books, 2002. All rights reserved.

Picture acknowledgments
Cover, 12, 18, 22, 28: The Image Bank.
6, 14, 16, 26: SuperStock Ltd. 10: Powerstock Zefa.

Text acknowledgments
Matthew 6:25–30, 32, 34 (abridged), from
the *Holy Bible, New International Version*, copyright
© 1973, 1978, 1984 by International Bible Society.
Used by permission.

DO NOT WORRY
Copyright © 2002 by Good Books, Intercourse, PA 17534
International Standard Book Number: 1-56148-364-8
Library of Congress Catalog Card Number: 2002024490

Printed and bound in Singapore.

Library of Congress Cataloging-in-Publication Data
Do not worry.
    p.cm.
    ISBN: 1-56148-364-8
    1. Bible. N.T. Matthew VI, 25-34--Devotional literature.
I. Good Books (Intercourse, Pa.)
BS2575.54.D6 2002
242'.5--dc21   2002024490

do not worry

Good Books

Intercourse, PA 17534
800/762-7171 • www.goodbks.com

I know not what
you believe of God,
but I believe he
gave yearnings and
longings to be filled,
and that he did not
mean all our time
should be devoted
to feeding and
clothing the body.

Lucy Stone

Do not worry
about your life,
what you will eat or drink;
or about your body,
what you will wear.

Is not life more important than food, and the body more important than clothes?

Everybody's got a hungry heart.

Bruce Springsteen

There must be more to life than having everything.

Maurice Sendak

Man cannot live by bread alone.
He must have peanut butter.

Dave Gardner

Look
at the birds of   the air;
          they do not sow

or reap

or store away in barns,
and yet
your heavenly
Father feeds
them.

People wish to be settled:

only as far as they are unsettled

is there any hope for them.

Ralph Waldo Emerson

The world is too much with us;

late and soon, getting and spending,

we lay waste our powers.

William Wordsworth

Are you not much more valuable than they?

Imagine that you are a masterpiece unfolding, every second of every day.

Thomas Crum

We are each so much more than what some reduce to measuring. Karen Kaiser Clark

The mind is its own place, and in itself can make a Heav'n of Hell, a Hell of Heav'n.

John Milton

I've developed a new philosophy... I only dread one day at a time.

Charles Schulz

by worrying
can add a
single hour
to his life?

And why do you worry about clothes?

One day our descendants will think it incredible that we paid so much attention to things like the amount of melanin in our skin or the shape of our eyes or our gender instead of the unique identities of each of us as complex human beings.

Franklin Thomas

See how the lilies
of the field grow.
They do not labor
or spin.

To me the meanest flower

that blows can give

Thoughts that do often lie

too deep for tears.

William Wordsworth

If you want to test your memory,

try to recall

what you were worrying about

one year ago today.

Author unknown

Yet I tell you that not even Solomon

There's never a new fashion but it's old.

Geoffrey Chaucer

was dressed like one of these.

God has been so lavish in his gifts that you can lose some priceless ones, the equivalent of whole kingdoms, and still be indecently rich.

Wilfrid Heed

in all his splendor

There is sublime thieving in all giving.

Someone gives us all he has and we are his.

Eric Hoffer

If that is how God clothes the grass of the field, which is here today and tomorrow is thrown into the fire,

I find it interesting that the meanest life, the poorest existence, is attributed to God's will, but as human beings become more affluent, as their living standard and style begin to ascend the material scale, God descends the scale of responsibility at a commensurate speed.

Maya Angelou

If we really
think about it,
God exists
for any
single individual
who puts his
trust in him,
not for the
whole of
humanity,
with its laws,
its organizations,
and its violence.

Salvatore Satta

*will
he not
much
more
clothe
you,*

Worry is a
thin stream
of fear
trickling
through the
mind.
If encouraged,
it cuts a
channel into
which all
the other
thoughts
are drained.

Arthur Somers Roche

O you of little faith?

Your heavenly
Father knows
that you need
all these things.

Have patience with everything that remains
unsolved in your heart. Try to love the questions
themselves, like locked rooms and like books
written in a foreign language.

Rainer Maria Rilke

We know what we are,

but know not what we may be.

William Shakespeare

 Therefore

It is always sunrise somewhere.

John Muir

do not
worry
about
tomorrow.

Do not worry about your life, what you will eat or drink; or about your body, what you will wear. Is not life more important than food, and the body more important than clothes? Look at the birds of the air; they do not sow or reap or store away in barns, and yet your heavenly Father feeds them. Are you not much more valuable than they? Who of you by worrying can add a single hour to his life?